Developing Li...
SPEAKING & LISTENING

PHOTOCOPIABLE ACTIVITIES
FOR THE LITERACY HOUR

year

Christine Moorcroft
and Ray Barker

A & C BLACK

Contents

Acknowledgements
The authors and publishers are grateful for permission to reproduce the following:
p. 21 'Some Favourite Words' by Richard Edwards, reproduced by kind permission of the author.
First published in *Whispers from a Wardrobe*, Lutterworth Press, 1987; p. 35 extract from *Sally Cinderella* by Bernard Ashley, first published
in the UK by Orchard Books in 1996, a division of the Watts publishing Group Limited, 96 Leonard Street, London EC2A 4XD; p. 45 'A Smile'
by Jez Alborough, reproduced by kind permission of the author. First published in *Whispers from a Wardrobe*, Lutterworth Press, 1987.
Every effort has been made to trace copyright holders and to obtain their permission for use of copyright material. The authors and publishers
would be pleased to rectify in future editions any error or omission.

Published 2006 by A & C Black Publishers Limited
38 Soho Square, London W1D 3HB
www.acblack.com

ISBN-10: 0-7136-7371-0
ISBN-13: 978-0-7136-7371-5

Copyright text © Christine Moorcroft, 2006
Copyright illustrations © Lynn Breeze, 2006
Copyright cover illustration © Andy Robb, 2006
Editors: Lynne Williamson and Marie Lister
Designer: Heather Billin

The authors and publishers would like to thank Fleur Lawrence and Kim Perez for their advice in producing this series of books.
A CIP catalogue record for this book is available from the British Library.
Printed and bound in Great Britain by Cromwell Press Ltd, Trowbridge, Wiltshire.

A & C Black uses paper produced with elemental chlorine-free pulp, harvested from managed sustainable forests.

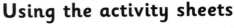

Developing Literacy: Speaking and Listening is a series of seven photocopiable activity books for the Literacy Hour. Each book provides a range of speaking and listening activities and supports the teaching and learning objectives identified in *Curriculum Guidance for the Foundation Stage* and by the Primary National Strategy in *Speaking, Listening, Learning: working with children in Key Stages 1 and 2.*

Speaking and listening skills are vital to children's intellectual and social development, particularly in helping them to:

- develop creativity;
- interact with others;
- solve problems;
- speculate and discourse;
- form social relationships;
- build self-confidence.

The activities in this book focus on the following four aspects of speaking and listening:

- **Speaking:** being able to speak clearly; developing and sustaining ideas in talk
- **Listening:** developing active listening strategies; using skills of analysis
- **Group discussion and interaction:** taking different roles in groups; working collaboratively; making a range of contributions
- **Drama:** improvisation; working in role; scripting and performing; responding to performances

Using the activity sheets

The materials show how speaking and listening can be relevant to all parts of literacy lessons, in whole-class work, in group or paired work, during independent work and in plenary sessions. The activities encourage the inclusion of all learners, since talking and contributing to group work are often more accessible than writing for lower-achieving children and for those who speak English as an additional language.

Extension activities

Most of the activity sheets end with a challenge (**Now try this!**), which reinforces and extends the children's learning and provides the teacher with an opportunity for assessment. These more challenging activities might be appropriate for only a few children; it is not expected that the whole class should complete them. For most of the extension activities, the children will need a notebook or a separate sheet of paper.

Organisation

Few resources are needed besides scissors, glue, word banks and simple dictionaries. Access to ICT resources – computers, video, tape recorders – will also be useful at times. To help teachers select appropriate learning experiences for their pupils, the activities are grouped into sections within the book. The pages need not be presented in the order in which they appear, unless stated otherwise. The sheets are intended to support, rather than direct, the teacher's planning.

Brief notes are provided at the bottom of each page, giving ideas and suggestions for making the most of the activity sheet. They may include suggestions for a whole-class introduction, a plenary session or follow-up work. These notes may be masked before photocopying if desired. More detailed notes and suggestions can be found on pages 6–8.

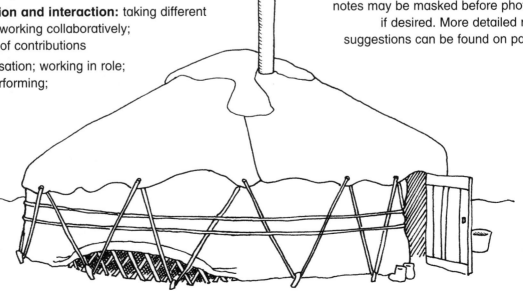

Effective group work

Many of the activities involve children working in groups. Here are some ideas to consider as you prepare for group work.

Before you start

HOW?

- How are deadlines and groupings made clear to groups?
- How might different children undertake different tasks?
- How will you organise time and space to give children the opportunity to rehearse and practise new skills?
- How will the children reflect on what they have learned about talk and its impact?

WHEN?

- When is working in a group appropriate?
- When is speaking and listening the focus of an activity?
- When is speaking and listening the outcome?
- When is it right for one child to become an 'expert' and inform others?

WHERE?

- Where in the class is the work going to take place in order to give space and manage noise levels?
- Where is it best for you to be to monitor the groups?
- Where might group work result in a finished product, such as a leaflet, and what resources will you need?

Tips for grouping children

- Be clear about the nature and purpose of the task.
- Decide which type of grouping is best for your purpose (pairs, attainment groups, friendship groups).
- Consider the advantages of mixed- or single-sex groupings in your particular class.
- Consider how you will include all abilities in these groups.
- Think carefully about who will lead groups and how you can vary this.
- Aim to vary the experience for the children: for example, using different groupings, ways of recording or learning environments. Experiment with what works best for different kinds of learners.

Your role

The notes in this book suggest an active role for you as a teacher, and give examples of how you can develop children's learning. Your role will vary from activity to activity, but here are some general points to bear in mind when working with children on speaking and listening activities:

- Be challenging in your choice of topics.
- Don't be afraid to use the correct language for talk: for example, *dialogue, gesture, narrator, negotiate, open and closed questions* and so on.
- Set the ground rules: everyone has a right to speak but everyone also has a duty to listen to others, take turns and so on.
- Move around to monitor what is happening in the groups. You can move on group discussions by developing and questioning what the children say.
- Provide models of the patterns of language expected for particular kinds of speech.
- Try to steer children away from using closed questions.
- Ensure children give extended answers and always ask them to explain their thinking.
- Allow children time to formulate their responses and treat everyone's responses with respect – but avoid praising every answer.

Assessment

An assessment sheet is provided on page 48 for children to assess their own progress. The children can complete the sheet on their own or in discussion with you. It is not expected that you will be able to assess the entire class at any one time. It is best to focus on a small group of children each week, although whole-class monitoring may be possible with certain activities, such as drama activities where children perform to the whole class.

Other activities in the book are ideal for the collection of evidence over the year (for example, *Fizz bomb, Home from home: 1, Packing to go, Video watch, In the news, Scene to scene*) and for children to assess one another's skills in speaking and listening (*The Ark, The Wind and the Sun, A question of magic, Voice-over, The root of the matter, I am the greatest!*). All the information should be assimilated for an end-of-year summary to facilitate target setting and the transition to Year 4.

Speaking

The activities in this section provide contexts to encourage the children to speak clearly, audibly and with control to a partner, another adult, their group or the class and to be aware of their audience.

Fizz bomb (page 9). In this activity the children work in pairs to explain a science experiment. When vinegar (an acid) is mixed with bicarbonate of soda (a base), the acid–base reaction makes the bottle fill with bubbles full of carbon dioxide, which in turn forces the cork out of the bottle. At the end of the lesson, make a fizz bomb for the class, inviting children to tell you what to do. The children could first discuss and agree safety rules. *Health and safety: Close supervision is required to ensure that the cork cannot hit anyone's face. An adult should fit the cork as soon as the vinegar has been added to the bicarbonate of soda. The experiment is messy and should be done outdoors.* **Vocabulary:** after that, before, discuss, explain, first, listen, next, notes, order, sequence, speak, then.

Home from home: 1 and 2 (pages 10–11). Here the children plan a talk about yurts. Discuss how to engage an audience in the opening sentence of a talk through the use of evocative phrases, such as 'on the roof of the world', 'on windswept mountain plains'. The opening should make a link with something the audience knows about. Explain the purpose of a summary: to remind the audience of the main points. Discuss how this kind of talk differs from telling a story: it is a report in the present tense and its purpose is to give information in a logical order, whereas a story is told in the past tense with the events in chronological order. Provide opportunities for the children to give their talks. They could enlarge and display the picture and point to the parts they are talking about. **Vocabulary:** audience, caption, conclusion, information, introduction, summary.

Knock, knock (page 12). This helps the children to use their voices and other sounds effectively. The children could make their own collection of jokes and practise telling them. **Vocabulary:** aggressively, angrily, bad-tempered, gently, joke, sing-song, sound, sound effect.

De Bottleman (page 13). Ask the children if they know what a 'bottleman' is. They can find out from the poem. Children from the Caribbean might be familiar with the sound and sight of a bottleman (or have heard about them from members of their families). **Vocabulary:** call, dialect, recite, sound, voice.

The Ark (page 14). This story is derived from 'Why Noah Chose the Dove' (Isaac Bashevis Singer, from *The Kingfisher Treasury of Stories for Seven Year Olds*). Ask the children to consider what the horse, cow, bee and fish might say. (Does the fish need to go into the Ark? What might it say?) Allow opportunities for the children to perform their stories to the class. **Vocabulary:** boast, brag, loudly, show off, stress, tone of voice, volume.

The Wind and the Sun (page 15). This fable offers opportunities to use sound effects, such as the wind blowing. The children could produce sounds using their voices. **Vocabulary:** boast, bullying, coaxing, fable, force, forceful, gentle, loud, moral, narrator, persuasion, persuasive, power, powerful, quiet, tone of voice, volume.

Food guards (page 16). In this activity the children find out how different foods are good for us and about any damage they can do. The activity supports work in science and citizenship (democracy and voting). Point out that the children will need to sound convincing in order to persuade their group. Model how to use your voice persuasively. **Vocabulary:** choice, choose, convince, explain, listen, persuade, voice, vote.

Packing to go (page 17). The children could first discuss in pairs what they would not want to leave behind. They could begin with a long list and then eliminate items. Ask them to tell their partner why some items are more important to them than others. **Vocabulary:** choice, choose, explain, reason, role-play.

Tell me more (page 18). This can support work in citizenship on choices, understanding right and wrong and the work of the police. Ask what people should do if they witness a theft. What difference does it make if the thief is a friend? Invite volunteers to contribute to a list of courses of action which they think are right and which also help the friend. **Vocabulary:** ask, choose, conversation, explain, listen, opinion, question, right, said, says, speak, views, wrong.

Listening

These activities develop children's skills as active listeners and help them to join in meaningful discussions. Demonstrate what is meant by good listening by enlisting the help of another adult for a short role-play of bad listening (fidgeting, looking away from the speaker, interrupting, daydreaming and so on). Ask the children to say what is wrong and what the listener should do instead.

The mystery (page 19). The story could be continued in a literacy lesson as a shared writing task for groups or the whole class. **Vocabulary:** agree, beginning, disagree, discuss, listen, mystery, opening, spider chart.

A question of magic (page 20). Children who undertake the extension activity should invite feedback from other groups before the class takes a vote. During the plenary, ask whether anyone changed their mind during the discussion, and why. **Vocabulary:** agree, convince, disagree, discuss, discussion, feedback, listen, vote.

Favourite words (page 21). Encourage the children to ask one another what they like about the sound of a word they choose: they might like the repeated 'u' sound in 'mugwump' or the onomatopoeia of 'swizzle', 'wallow', 'ooze' or 'lush'. **Vocabulary**: agree, convince, disagree, discuss, discussion, favourite, listen, onomatopoeia.

Pictures and sounds (page 22). Ask the children what they learn from the images and sounds, and what effect is created. For the extension activity, the children will need to watch the video again with the sound turned off. **Vocabulary**: image, music, picture, screen, sound, voice.

In the news (page 23). To appreciate the contribution of visual images, the children could first listen to the news bulletin without looking at the screen. Discuss to what extent they depend on visual images. Compare this with radio news, in which sound has to stand alone. **Vocabulary**: diagram, effect, information, map, media, moving picture, news, newsreader, sound, still picture, voice.

Toddlers' TV (page 24). To help with identifying presentational features, you could ask the children to listen to a story from the radio and to identify when they hear all the key features: theme music, other music, voices, sound effects. **Vocabulary**: broadcast, image, picture, programme, radio, scene, sound, television.

Beginning, middle and ending (page 25). First discuss the structure of a feature film. To make sense to a viewer, there has to be an introduction before the main part of the story. Here the audience learns the names of the characters and begins to identify them. The story develops during the middle section and then comes a conclusion in which problems are resolved (or, if it is a serial, there might be a 'cliffhanger'). **Vocabulary**: animation, beginning, character, cliffhanger, drama, enact, ending, middle, narrator, order, presenter, sequence, serial.

Voice-over (page 26). Once the children have matched the voice-overs to the pictures, discuss how the visual images support the information given in the voice-overs. **Vocabulary**: broadcast, image, order, presenter, sequence, shot, sketch, visual, voice-over.

Magnetic mix-up (page 27). After the children have arranged the scenes in order, ask which words helped them to link the scenes. Draw attention to time sequencing ('later'), referring back to something which has just been mentioned ('here'), preparing to give information by asking a question ('So how does it work?') and signalling an answer ('Well – '). **Vocabulary**: connect, link, music, order, sequence, sound, voice-over.

Scene to scene (page 28). This focuses on scene changes in an information programme. You could stop the video just after the first two or three scene changes and discuss the words and phrases used by the presenter to signal the change. **Vocabulary**: connect, connective, link, presenter, scene, sequence, sound, voice-over.

Group discussion and interaction

In these activities the children use talk to explore and share ideas, and they collaborate in activities, such as solving a problem. The children take different roles in groups: for example, suggesting ideas, acting as scribe, and asking questions for information or clarification.

The root of the matter (page 29). Before writing notes the children should wait for each speaker to finish, or one child could act as scribe. They should write only the main points, briefly explaining what to do. The children should listen to the ideas of each member of their group before discussing the merits of each one and deciding which will best help them to answer the question. They can then decide who will do what. Help them to rotate tasks such as writing, fetching equipment and tidying up during the course of a week. **Vocabulary**: answer, ask, discuss, listen, notes, question, take turns.

Jumble sale (page 30). This provides opportunities to include work in citizenship and mathematics. Discuss the children's experiences of jumble sales and identify the tasks which had to be carried out before, during and after the event: choosing a time, date and place, and notifying people so that they can donate goods and attend the event; organising furniture and containers for money; deciding what should be sold and on how many different stalls; allocating helpers to the stalls, thanking them and letting them know how much money was raised and how it was spent. For the extension activity, you could help the children to plan using a diary or calendar in order to identify deadlines for each task. **Vocabulary**: allocate, choose, identify, list, organise, rota, task.

Egg challenge: 1 and 2 (pages 31–32). In this activity the children use and develop literacy skills (scanning and skimming texts and making notes) as they carry out research tasks. During one lesson the children could discuss the challenge and who will do each piece of research, and carry out their research. They could then present reports to their groups during another lesson. Encourage volunteers to present their reports to the class during the plenary session, when you could also discuss how the containers could be put to the test and how to choose which ones to post. Point out that the consideration of cost needs to be balanced against the effectiveness of the container. **Vocabulary**: ask, design, eye contact, listen, main points, notes, present, presentation, question, report, research, share, speak, task.

A good discussion (page 33). Ask the children how the behaviour of the others in the group might affect how Ellie feels about making a presentation to them. Discuss which of them encourage her and how: for example, using her name and asking questions. The extension activity links with text-level work on writing letters. **Vocabulary**: ask, discussion, eye contact, listen, present, presentation, question, report, speak.

This is the greatest! (page 34). After each speaker has presented their argument, the others may challenge what has been said: for example, one speaker might argue that without light bulbs people would not be able to see at night; another may respond that fire is more important because it not only provides light, but also gives out heat for warmth and for cooking. Draw out that a challenge is neither a confrontation nor an attack, but shows that the other person has been listening; a challenge can also help the speaker to express ideas more clearly. **Vocabulary:** ask, challenge, eye contact, listen, notes, present, presentation, question, speak, vote.

Story characters: 1 and 2 (pages 35–36). After reading the passage, discuss what is meant by 'treating others well'. Ask the children whether Sally's mum is nice to her, and what she does or says that is not nice. (Point out how she speaks to Sally and draw attention to Sally's fears when she has not managed to get the cigarettes for her mother.) Discuss how this might affect Sally, drawing out that she does not feel confident with other people; she avoids looking at and speaking to people in the shop and she never smiles. The children should notice Kompel's gentle way of taking the note from Sally because she knows that Sally flinches at sudden movements. Discuss why. **Vocabulary:** affection, behaviour, care, character, feelings, friendship, relationship, respect.

What if…? (page 37). This activity develops the children's skills in using the language of possibility to investigate and reflect on feelings, behaviour or relationships. **Vocabulary:** because, character, choice, consequence, could, if, in case, maybe, might, possibly, should, so, then, whether, why, would.

Drama

These activities provide support for the children to use their voices, facial expressions and body movements to portray characters and to enact stories. The children are also encouraged to talk about the way in which a performance is enacted, saying what they enjoyed.

Guess who (page 38). Ask the children to think about how they will engage the interest of their audience. You could encourage them to treat this in a humorous way. **Vocabulary:** act, character, conversation, dialogue, role.

Digging up the past (page 39). This kind of activity could be linked with any period being studied by the children. If a mock dig is carried out, the children could photograph their 'finds' and import the photographs into a word-processed report about them, written during a literacy lesson. **Vocabulary:** act, answer, archaeologist, artefact, conversation, dialogue, enact, question, role-play.

Lost in the woods (page 40). Ask the children to consider whether their character might help the others or need help. Which character might become the leader of the group?

How might they support one another? What would be their strengths and weaknesses? Might some act selfishly? Would any character harm the others? Would any of them cause problems by accident? Allow opportunities for the children to perform their scenes. **Vocabulary:** act, character, conversation, dialogue, drama, personality, role, scene.

In the wrong (page 41). Here the children use drama techniques to explore why making the right choices is not always easy: for example, Lucy might not want to fall out with Patrick, she might be afraid to disagree with him or she might worry about doing something which she later regrets. **Vocabulary:** act, agree, bullying, dialogue, disagree, drama, fair, friend, right, role-play, scene, unfair, wrong.

Costume drama (page 42). Begin by showing the children a photograph of a character from a film and asking them what his/her clothes tell them about the character. **Vocabulary:** audience, character, clothes, costume, drama, wardrobe.

Actions speak louder (page 43). While watching a video you could stop at different points and ask the children to mime the gestures and actions of one of the characters. Discuss what the character was doing and the emotions involved. **Vocabulary:** action, character, emotion, gesture, mime, portray, scene.

Face to face (page 44). This could be linked with work in art on portraits. The children could label copies of works of art according to what they think the person feels. To support work in history, they could make Greek theatre masks to be worn during performances of Greek myths. **Vocabulary:** action, character, drama, emotion, facial expression, feeling, mask, theatre.

Pass it on (page 45). This can be used to support work in citizenship (taking part in a community) and in assemblies (friendship and community). **Vocabulary:** community, emotion, expression, feeling, influence, issue, verse.

Abraham and Sarah (page 46). After reading the passage, discuss the possible responses of Abraham: sadness at the idea of leaving his home and family, or pride and honour at having been chosen to be the father of a great nation. Then talk about how Sarah might have felt. **Vocabulary:** act, dialogue, faith, feelings, respond, response, scene.

Victims (page 47). After the children have completed the main activity, invite feedback and draw out the possible consequences for the victim, apart from the loss of their property. **Vocabulary:** dialogue, emotions, event, feelings, issue, monologue, role, role-play.

How did you do? (page 48). This is a simple self-assessment sheet. It is not intended for use after every activity, but should be given when it is felt appropriate. Sections not applicable to the activity can be masked.

Fizz bomb

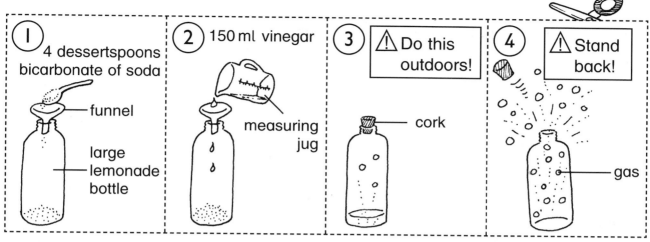

1. 4 dessertspoons bicarbonate of soda — funnel — large lemonade bottle
2. 150 ml vinegar — measuring jug
3. ⚠ Do this outdoors! — cork
4. ⚠ Stand back! — gas

- **Work with a partner. Together you are going to explain how to make a fizz bomb.**

☆ Your teacher will give you two cards each.

☆ Take turns to describe what is happening on your cards.
  Your partner should make notes on the notepad.

☆ Start with card ①.

How to _make a fizz bomb_ _____

Safety rules _____

Equipment _____

Stages

① _____

② _____

③ _____

④ What happens? _____

Now try this!

- **Discuss what made the cork shoot out.**
- **Explain your ideas to another pair.**

Teachers' note This activity could be introduced during a science lesson (exploring the ways in which materials behave when mixed). Make a copy of this page for each pair and cut out the cards. Give cards 1 and 3 to child A, and cards 2 and 4 to child B. Child A explains stage 1 and child B makes notes on the notepad, then they swap roles for each subsequent stage, using the same notepad.

Developing Literacy
Speaking & Listening
Year 3
© A & C BLACK

Home from home: 1

- **Look at the picture of a** [yurt]**.**
  Read the caption and labels.
- **Plan a talk about yurts.**

Write notes.

Introduction

Make the audience want to listen.

What is a yurt?

Description

Where is a yurt used?

What is special about it?

Summary

Sum up the main points.

Now try this!

- **Collect information about another type of home.**
- **Use a chart like this to plan a talk about it.**

Teachers' note Use this with page 11. Ask the children to find out as much as possible about yurts from the picture. They could also use the Internet for research. Help the children to identify the important features of a yurt. They should make notes which will help them to tell others about yurts.

**Developing Literacy
Speaking & Listening
Year 3
© A & C BLACK**

Home from home: 2

Roof covered with canvas or burlap (a type of felt). It can be rolled up and packed on a camel.

Strong ropes to tie down the cover and bind it to the walls.

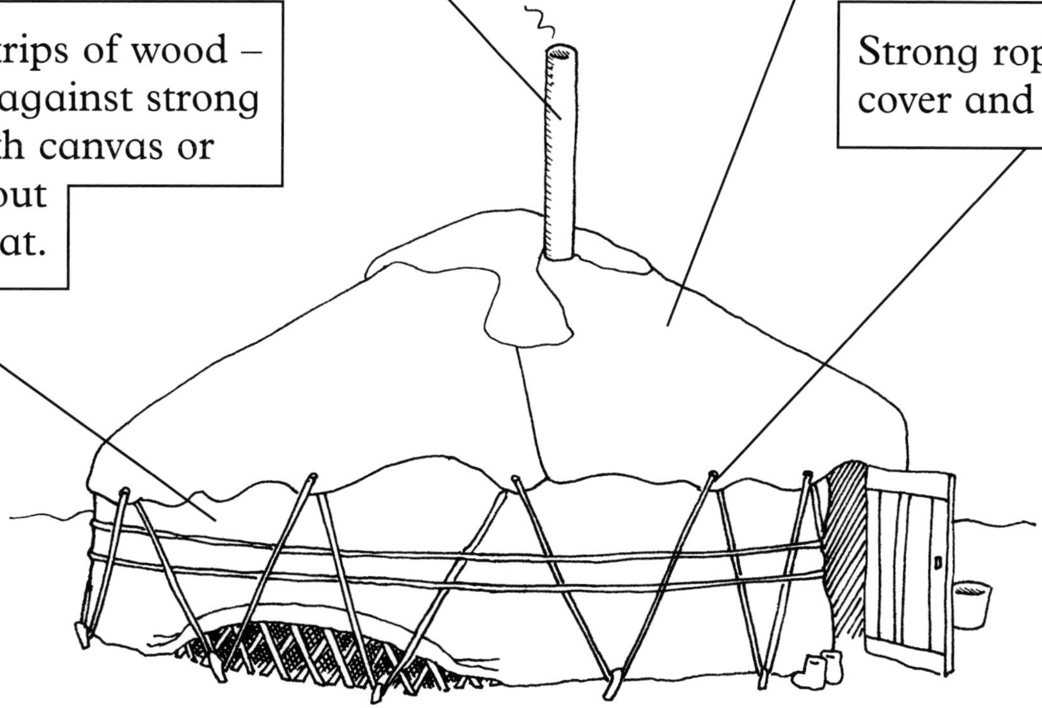

Tall metal pipe used as a chimney. Fires burn wood and peat.

Walls made from strips of wood – woven for strength against strong winds – covered with canvas or burlap. They keep out the cold and the heat.

A yurt

Travelling people of Mongolia set up yurts as homes. Mongolia is a high, mountainous country with hot summers and very cold winters. Winds can be very strong there.

Teachers' note Use this with page 10. The picture shows a yurt – a traditional dwelling of nomadic herders from the mountainous areas in and around Mongolia. In addition to the opportunities offered for speaking and listening, this page can be used to introduce work in geography (Passport to the world).

Developing Literacy
Speaking & Listening
Year 3
© A & C BLACK

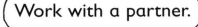

Knock, knock

☆ Cover the notepaper.

☆ Take turns to read out the lines in each joke.

☆ Uncover the notepaper.

☆ Read out the jokes again, using the notes.

☆ Talk about the difference.

 Work with a partner.

Knock, knock.
Who's there?
Thea.
Thea who?
Thea later, alligator.

Say it as if knocking on a door.
Call out. Make 'there' long.
Call out.
Make it sound like a question.
Use a sing-song voice.

Knock, knock.
Who's there?
Joanna.
Joanna who?
Joanna smack?

Say it as if knocking angrily.
Sound bad-tempered.
Call out.
Sound bad-tempered.
Say it as if you are looking
for a fight!

 Now try this!

- **Write another 'knock, knock' joke.**
- **Make notes about how to read it.**

Teachers' note Once the children have read the jokes, model different ways of reading each line and ask them which they think sounds the best. Then discuss the notes on the notepaper: for example, how the children can sound as if they are knocking gently and how they should call out. They could also use sound effects such as knocking on a table top (gently or aggressively).

**Developing Literacy
Speaking & Listening
Year 3
© A & C BLACK**

De Bottleman

- **Read the poem.**
- **Make notes about how to recite it. The notes have been started for you.**

Work with a partner.

De Bottleman

Bottles! Bottles!
Bottles I buy. →

Call out loudly

Hear de bottleman cry ←

Say it quickly and quietly

Long bottles
Short bottles
Fat bottles
Thin bottles ←

Bottles! Bottles!
Bottles I buy. ←

Hear de bottleman cry ←

Search low search high. ←

I buy dem wet
I buy dem dry ←

Run with a bottle
to de bottleman cart
when yuh hear de bottleman cry ←

Bottles! Bottles!
Bottles I buy. ←

John Agard

Now try this!

- **Recite the poem to another pair.**
- **Mark anything you need to read differently.**

Teachers' note Model how to read the bottleman's cry (as if calling out from the street to people indoors). Help the children to distinguish between what he calls out and how it is described, and discuss how punctuation could help. The children could mark commas, full stops and speech marks. Discuss why some of the words are not spelled as the children might expect: *de* (the), *yuh* (you).

Developing Literacy
Speaking & Listening
Year 3
© A & C BLACK

13

The Ark

- **Work in a group.**
- **Read the story.**
- **Continue the story.**

Think about how each animal might sound.

They say that there's going to be a flood. We'll all drown.

Noah's building an ark. He's going to choose the best animals to take in.

He'll take me – I'm king of the beasts.

I can lay eggs for him.

I am a man's best friend.

Now try this!

- **What do you think Noah did? Discuss the end of the story and decide what happened.**

Teachers' note Remind the children of the Bible story of Noah and the Ark (Genesis 6–9) and explain that this is a version of the story in which the animals compete with one another to show why they should be taken into the Ark. Discuss how to read the words of the animals to sound boastful. Which words will be stressed? Encourage the children to use expression, volume and tone of voice effectively.

Developing Literacy Speaking & Listening Year 3 © A & C BLACK

The Wind and the Sun

• **Read the** | fable |**.**

(Work with a partner.)

The Wind and the Sun

One day the Wind and the Sun had a quarrel.

'I am much stronger than you,' boasted the Wind.

'I think you are wrong,' said the Sun.

'Let's put it to the test,' said the Wind. 'Do you see that man travelling along the road? Let's see who can get his cloak off his back.'

'As you like,' replied the Sun. 'You may begin.'

So the Wind blew and blew as hard as it could. The Wind had blown down buildings but it could not take off the man's cloak. The harder it blew, the more tightly the man wrapped his cloak around him.

'Well, you cannot be stronger than that,' said the Wind, 'but you might as well try.'

So the Sun shone brightly and the weather became warmer. The man smiled and relaxed. The Sun shone more strongly. The man got hotter. His face became red. He mopped his brow. He was so hot that he stopped for a rest. He took off his cloak and spread it on the ground to sit on.

• **Describe the voices of the Wind and the Sun.**

Wind	**Sun**
_____	_____
_____	_____
_____	_____
_____	_____

Word bank

bullying   loud
coaxing   persuasive
forceful   powerful
gentle   quiet

• **Practise reading the fable together. Use your voices to show what the Wind and the Sun are like.**

Now try this!

• **Read the fable aloud to another pair.**
• **Explain the** | moral | **of the fable.**

Teachers' note Explain that a fable is a story, often about animals, which is told to teach people something about human nature or to encourage them to improve their behaviour. Draw out that the Wind is showing off about its power. Discuss how the children should speak the parts of the two characters and the narrator (explain this term, if necessary), and where their voices should change.

**Developing Literacy
Speaking & Listening
Year 3
© A & C BLACK**

Food guards

- **Choose a 'good-for-you' food from the list. Find out as much as you can about it.**
- **Plan a talk to tell the food guards why it should be allowed into the kitchen.**

KITCHEN

Stop! Only 'good-for-you' foods are allowed.

Notes for my talk

Food _____

Why I chose it

- _____
- _____
- _____
- _____
- _____
- _____

Foods
avocado
banana
bread
cheese
chips
chocolate
ice cream
jam
milk
orange
peanut butter
sprouts
toffee

- **Explain why you chose this food. Your group should vote** yes **or** no **on whether to let it into the kitchen.**

Work in a group.

Now try this!

- **Together, choose a food which should not be let in. Write five reasons to explain why.**

Teachers' note The children will need access to information books, leaflets and websites about food and nutrition. Ask them, working individually, to make notes on the chart about why the food guards should allow their chosen food into the kitchen: for example, it is tasty, nutritious (in what way?), cheap and so on. The children then take turns to explain to the rest of the group, who act as 'food guards'.

Developing Literacy
Speaking & Listening
Year 3
© A & C BLACK

Packing to go

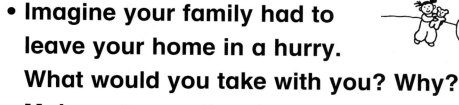

- **Imagine your family had to leave your home in a hurry.**
  What would you take with you? Why?
- **Make notes on the chart.**

Apart from clothes, you can take:
a book, a toy or game and one other thing.

My choices	Reasons
Book	
Toy or game	
Other	

- **Explain your choices to the rest of the group.**

Now try this!

- **What if a parent or carer wanted to stop you taking these things? Role-play what they might say and what you would say.**

Work with a partner.

Teachers' note First read some accounts of families who have had to flee their homes with a limited amount of luggage, such as *When Hitler Stole Pink Rabbit* by Judith Kerr. Draw out that these people could take only the most important things with them. The children could discuss in pairs which objects are important to them. (Tell them that all family members and pets will be taken.)

Developing Literacy
Speaking & Listening
Year 3
© A & C BLACK

Tell me more

- **Work with a partner.**
- **Ask your partner this question:**

 What should you do if you see a friend stealing?

- **Make notes about what your partner says.**

  Ask more questions to keep your partner talking.

You should _____

_____

because _____ Why…?

_____

_____

_____

_____ How…?

_____

_____

_____ What…?

_____

_____

Now try this!

- **Explain your partner's view to the group.**

Teachers' note Explain that in this activity the children are going to encourage a partner to talk about his or her views by listening and asking questions. One child should find out the other's views, then they should swap roles. Remind them about good listening skills (see page 6). Point out the question words in the speech bubbles and how these are useful for finding information during conversations.

**Developing Literacy
Speaking & Listening
Year 3
© A & C BLACK**

- **Read this story opening.**
  What could be happening?

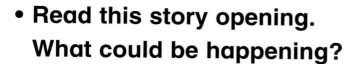

Work in a group of four.

Dilip rubbed his nose where it had hit the door.

'What's wrong, Dil?' asked his friend Amy, who was halfway through the doorway.

'Bashed my nose on the door,' he said, as he took another step. The same happened again.

They watched the rest of the class going through the doorway.

'What's going on?' asked Mr Bloom.

'I can't get through the door,' said Dilip.

'Nonsense. In you come,' said Mr Bloom.

Dilip tried again, with his hands in front of his face just in case. It felt as if the door were closed. Amy took his hand and pulled.

'Ouch!' she cried. 'How did I bump my elbow on air?'

- **Write everyone's ideas on the spider chart.**

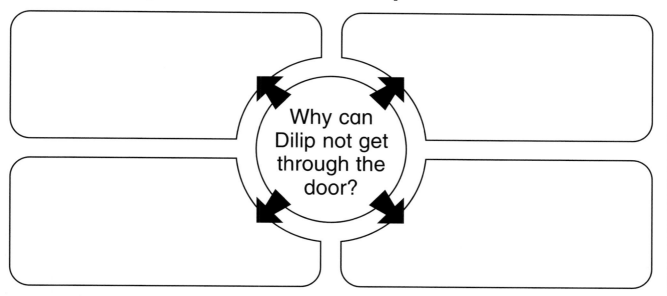

Why can Dilip not get through the door?

- **Discuss each idea. Do you agree or disagree?**

Now try this!

- **With your group, choose one idea and continue the story. Tell your story to another group.**

Teachers' note Encourage the children to work as a group, without adult intervention, unless they need help with reading the passage. Ensure they take turns to speak and listen to each other carefully. Point out that there is no 'right answer'. After they have completed the spider chart, invite feedback in a whole-class discussion. The class could vote for the best suggestion for continuing the story.

Developing Literacy
Speaking & Listening
Year 3
© A & C BLACK

A question of magic

- **Discuss this question:**

| Do you believe in magic? |

Work in a
group of four.

- **Write notes on the chart.**

Name	Yes or no	Why?

Now try
this!

- **Listen to what other groups say about magic.**
- **Have a vote to find out whether the class believes in magic.**

Teachers' note Read the question with the children and ask them to think about their answers and to consider the reasons for their beliefs. Give them time to think without speaking for a minute or two before they begin their group discussions. Ask each group to try to reach a decision about whether or not they believe in magic; the children could try to convince one another of their point of view.

**Developing Literacy
Speaking & Listening
Year 3
© A & C BLACK**

20

Favourite words

- **Read the poem.**

Work in a group.

Some Favourite Words

Mugwump, chubby, dunk and whoa,
Swizzle, doom and snoop,
Flummox, lilt and afterglow,
Gruff, bamboozle, whoop
And nincompoop.

Wallow, jungle, lumber, sigh,
Ooze and zodiac,
Innuendo, lullaby,
Ramp and mope and quack
And paddywhack.

Moony, undone, lush and bole,
Inkling, tusk, guffaw,
Waspish, croon and cubby-hole,
Fern, fawn, dumbledore
And many more …

Richard Edwards

- **Pick words from the poem and take turns to say them.**
- **Discuss which words your group likes the best. Write them here.**

_____

_____

_____

_____

 Now try this!

- **Make a list of your own favourite words to use in a class poem.**

Think of other words whose sounds you like.

_____   _____   _____

_____   _____   _____

_____   _____   _____

_____   _____   _____

- **As a class, write the poem.**

Teachers' note Tell the children that they are going to consider the sounds of the words rather than their meanings. (The meanings can be looked up afterwards.) Encourage children to use reading strategies developed in word-level work to help them read the words. For the extension activity, encourage the whole class to discuss and decide which words are the most effective.

Developing Literacy Speaking & Listening Year 3 © A & C BLACK

Pictures and sounds

Work with a partner.

- Watch an information video. What do you see and hear?
- Write about two different scenes.

Title

Scene (describe what you saw)	Sounds (describe what you heard)		
	Voices	Music	Other sounds

- What difference would it make if you could not hear the sound? Find out and describe it.

Now try this!

Teachers' note Show two or more scenes from an information programme. After the children have watched it for information, replay it and focus on how the information was presented. Discuss the images (which may include moving images, still photographs, drawings, diagrams and text) and sounds (including voices, music and sound effects).

Developing Literacy
Speaking & Listening
Year 3
© A & C BLACK

In the news

- Watch a television news story. How does it give the information?
- Make notes on the chart.

What I found out about the news story

What I heard and saw	What happened	Where it happened	When it happened	Who was in the story
Newsreader's voice				
Other voices				
Other sounds				
Diagrams and maps				
Still pictures				
Moving pictures				

- What is the main thing you remember about the story? Tell a partner.

Now try this!

Teachers' note Show the children a recorded television news story that makes use of most of the presentational features on the chart. They may need to watch it twice. During the second viewing you could stop at intervals and ask what the children saw and heard. Focus on the question words 'what?', 'where?', 'when?' and 'who?'

Developing Literacy
Speaking & Listening
Year 3
© A & C BLACK

Toddlers' TV

These scenes are from a television programme for very young children from 50 years ago.

• Cut out the cards.

• Match the sounds to the pictures.

Sounds

"He cut out the leather and set it out on his bench to sew the next day."	"It's about a poor shoemaker who had only enough leather for one pair of shoes."
"Welcome to Story Book. Let's see what today's story is."	Story Book theme music.

Pictures

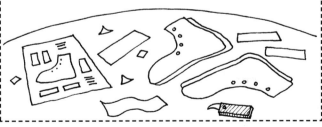

• **Watch a modern story programme for toddlers. Make notes about the first four scenes.**

Sounds	Pictures

Teachers' note Discuss how stories are presented on radio and television: are they enacted or read? Explain that in many of the earliest children's television programmes, stories were read in the same way as on radio, and sometimes pictures from the book were shown on the screen. Encourage the children to discuss how this compares with modern television programmes.

**Developing Literacy
Speaking & Listening
Year 3
© A & C BLACK**

Beginning, middle and ending

Films, like books, have:

 a beginning  a middle  an ending

 Work in a group.

- **Sort the cards to show which part they belong to.**

The main part of the story is acted.	We see different parts of the setting.	Music plays to set the scene.
Printed words tell parts of the story.	The title is shown on the screen.	A narrator tells parts of the story.
The main setting is introduced.	The characters face problems.	Music makes the story events more exciting.
The main characters are introduced.	The problems are worked out.	A list of all the people who worked on the film comes onto the screen.

 Now try this!

- **Tell a partner about your favourite part of a film. What did you see and hear?**

Teachers' note Copy the page onto card for each group. Show the first ten minutes of a feature film and discuss the structure of beginning, middle and ending. The children could draw three columns, headed 'Beginning', 'Middle' and 'Ending', on a sheet of paper. Ask them to discuss where they think each card belongs; some may fit into more than one column. Emphasise that the group has to agree.

**Developing Literacy
Speaking & Listening
Year 3
© A & C BLACK**

Voice-over

- **Cut out the cards.**
- **Match the** ⸢ voice-overs ⸣ **to the pictures.**
- **Glue them onto a chart like this:**

⸢ Work with a partner. ⸣

Pictures	Voice-overs

Pictures

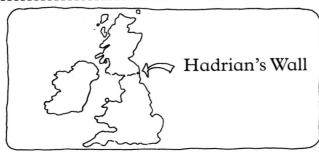

Hadrian's Wall

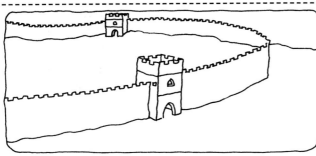

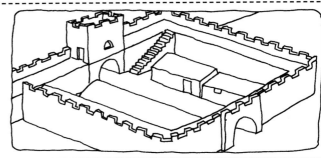

Voice-overs

> There were two **turrets** between each pair of milecastles. These were used as watchtowers.

> People could go through the wall at fortified gateways called **milecastles**. About 100 troops lived in each milecastle. They checked the people and goods going through.

> In AD 122 the Roman emperor Hadrian had a wall built across northern England. He wanted to control the people and goods going in and out of his empire.

> The Romans built several forts close to Hadrian's Wall. Some, like this one at Housesteads, were as big as towns and had many buildings. The troops here farmed and traded.

Now try this!

- **Think up a title for the video and sketch the first** ⸢ shot ⸣ **. Write a voice-over for it.**

Teachers' note Read out the voice-overs before giving the sheet to the children. Ask what the children learned and what else they want to know. Discuss the meanings of 'voice-over' and 'shot', and how a voice-over is different from having a presenter appearing on screen and speaking to the camera. Encourage the children to decide on the best order for the information, and to explain why.

Developing Literacy
Speaking & Listening
Year 3
© A & C BLACK

Magnetic mix-up

- ## Cut out the four strips.
- ## Put these scenes in order.

Work with a partner.

Pictures	Sounds	Voice-overs
	Sound of the sea. Sailors' voices. Ship's radio.	Later ships were built with their own compass, housed in a special case called a **binnacle**.
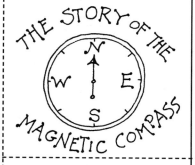	Music – 'La Mer' (The Sea) by Debussy	The magnetic compass – an instrument based on science known long ago. It began with an ore named **lodestone** or magnetite.
	No sound except the voice of the presenter.	Well – the Earth contains a huge mass of magnetic material close to the North Pole. Any piece of iron or iron ore has one end which is attracted by this huge mass.
	Sound of the sea. Sailors' voices.	Here we see a Norse sailor from about a thousand years ago using a lodestone to find North. So how does it work?

Now try this!

- ## Which words in the voice-over tell you that a new scene is starting? Underline them.

Teachers' note Make a copy of the page for each pair of children and ask them to cut out the cards along the *dotted* lines only (i.e. in horizontal strips). This enables them to move the scenes about physically to see whether the order makes sense.

Developing Literacy Speaking & Listening Year 3 © A & C BLACK

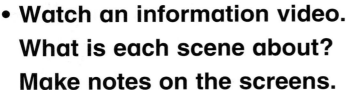 # Scene to scene

- **Watch an information video.**
  What is each scene about?
  Make notes on the screens.

 Work in a group.

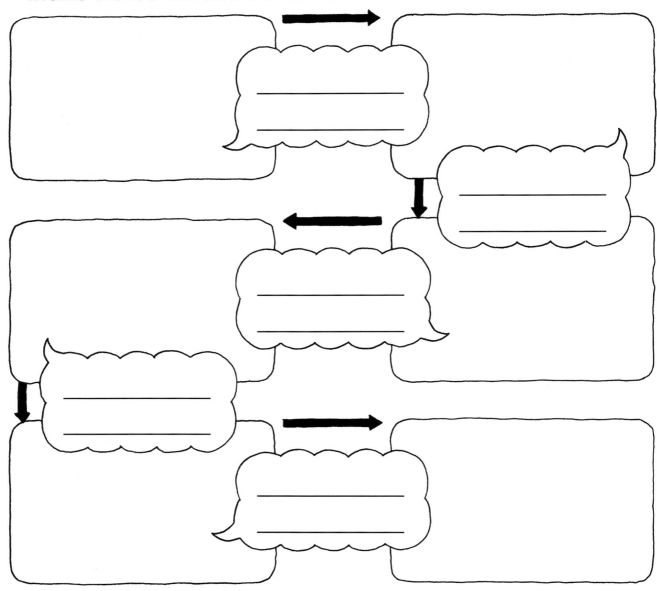

- **Watch the video again.**
  What does the presenter say to connect the scenes?
  Write the key words in the speech bubbles.

 Now try this!

- **Make a word bank of** connective **words you**
  hear in other videos and television programmes.

Teachers' note Split the class into groups and give each group a copy of this page. Show the children an information video (which could be linked with work in another subject). The first time they watch it, the children should write on the screens only. The second time, the children should listen for the words or phrases which indicate that a new scene is beginning, and write these in the bubbles.

Developing Literacy
Speaking & Listening
Year 3
© A & C BLACK

The root of the matter

- **Discuss this question.** Work in a group of four.

Can plants take in water without roots?

- **How can you find out the answer?**
  Listen to everyone's ideas.
  Make notes on the plant pots.

Who will do the writing?

- **What do you think will be the answer?**
  How will you know if you are right?
  What will you do? Who will do what?

- **Try out your experiment.**

Teachers' note Emphasise that everyone in the group should have an opportunity to speak and should listen carefully to each other's ideas. When it is their turn to speak, if someone else has had the same idea they can add to what has already been said.

Developing Literacy
Speaking & Listening
Year 3
© A & C BLACK

Jumble sale

Class 3 are having a jumble sale.

 We need to ask people to bring things to sell.

 Three people can look after each stall.

 We need tables.

- **What do the children need to do?**
  Talk to your group.
  Write a list.

Work in a group.

Jumble sale – things to do

_____

_____

_____

_____

_____

_____

_____

_____

_____

_____

_____

 Now try this!

- **What should the children do first?**
  Write out the list in the correct order.

Teachers' note This could be used in connection with any event the children are going to organise, such as a money-raising effort for charity. This provides support during the planning stage in which the children identify the tasks. During another lesson, the children could decide how to allocate the tasks among the class (see page 7).

**Developing Literacy
Speaking & Listening
Year 3
© A & C BLACK**

Egg challenge: 1

The great egg challenge is on!

Design a container to protect a hollow chocolate egg.
The test will be to post the egg.
It has to arrive unbroken.
Postage has to be cheap – so make
the container as light as possible.

- **First you need to do some research into containers.**

  Share these tasks. Find out about:

  - egg cartons

  - containers for chocolate eggs

  - materials used for packing

  - the mail (costs and what happens to parcels).

  > Work in a group of four.

  > Who will do what?

My task _____

Notes for my report _____

_____

_____

_____

_____

_____

_____

Now try this!

- **List the three most important points in your report.**
- **Explain to your group why these points are important.**

Teachers' note Use this with page 32. Each child needs a copy of both pages. This activity could be introduced during a design and technology lesson on the theme of 'containers'. Explain that, before designing a container to meet the challenge, the children should do some research and present their findings as a report. Discuss how and where they can find the information they need.

**Developing Literacy
Speaking & Listening
Year 3
© A & C BLACK**

Egg challenge: 2

- **Listen to one another's reports.**
- **List the main points.**
  Write the questions <u>you</u> asked.

Look at the speaker.
Ask questions.

Report about _____

by _____

Main points	Question
_____	_____
_____	_____
_____	_____

Report about _____

by _____

Main points	Question
_____	_____
_____	_____
_____	_____

Report about _____

by _____

Main points	Question
_____	_____
_____	_____
_____	_____

Now try this!

- **Use what you have learned to help you design an egg container.**

Teachers' note Use this with page 31. Model how to encourage a person to speak by inviting a volunteer to present his or her report to the class and afterwards, drawing attention to important points made by the speaker and asking questions to clarify points or to obtain further information. If possible, post the eggs to school to test the challenge: do any arrive unbroken?

Developing Literacy
Speaking & Listening
Year 3
© A & C BLACK

A good discussion

This group of children are having a discussion.
How well are they doing?

Harry

Ellie

Ellie, I'd like to know…

That was interesting, Ellie. Can you tell us more about…

I wonder what they are doing over there…

Sonali   Connor

- **Work with a partner.**
- **Fill in the report form.**

Discussion report		
Name	Good points	Bad points

Now try this!

- **Write a letter to the group.**
Tell them what they do well
and how they can improve.

Teachers' note Remind the children about how to hold a discussion and ask them to think about their rules for good discussions. The children should work in pairs and then share their responses with their groups or with the class. Discuss how the actions of the children in the picture help or hinder the discussion. Point out that boxes on the chart can be left blank if there are no obvious good/bad points.

Developing Literacy
Speaking & Listening
Year 3
© A & C BLACK

This is the greatest!

- ## Work in a large group.

☆ Cut out the cards.

☆ Put them in a pile, face down.

☆ Each pick up a card.

☆ Take turns to explain why this object is the most important.

A diamond is the most important because...

 a diamond	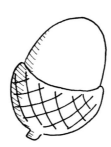 an acorn	 a light bulb
 a cloud	 a fire	 a pencil
 the moon	 a spade	a bag of flour

Now try this!

- ## Take a vote to decide which object is the most important.

Teachers' note Split the class into groups of up to nine and give each group two copies of this page. They should keep one copy intact to remind them of the objects in the collection. Give the children a few minutes to think about what they can say to show how important the object on their card is. They could make notes to help them.

**Developing Literacy
Speaking & Listening
Year 3
© A & C BLACK**

Story characters: 1

- **Read this passage from *Sally Cinderella* with your group.**

Sally Lane knew more about pavements than she did about the sky, knew tree roots better than the leaves. A smile for her would have worked muscles that hurt. It wasn't the same for her sisters – it wasn't the same for the dog – but that's how it was for Sally.

She was up and dressed and down at the shop before most of the others had opened their eyes.

"Fags," her mother said one morning, "an' sugar." She gave her no money, just pressed her pencil message into a soft piece of cardboard: soft-looking words, hard heart, because her mother knew that certain stupid people felt sorry for Sally Lane. She was always the one to send when she wasn't going to pay.

Mrs Vasisht was one of them: and so was Kompel, who helped in the shop when she wasn't at school. Sally was only six but everyone seemed to know her.

"Yeah?" Kompel asked as the thin little girl slid in round the door.

Sally gave up the note, her eyes as usual on the floor. Kompel took it gently – because a quick moving arm would make her flinch, she knew.

"Hang on. I'll have to ask."

Sally waited. She was used to this. Not paying usually meant a bit of a fuss. She yawned, eyed the fresh bread, smelt its heat.

"Sorry, tell your mother no cigarettes." Mrs Vasisht had come out. "Sugar O.K., but no cigarettes." She waved her fingers in a 'no' sign. "Cigarettes only for grown-ups. Little children not allowed." The shopkeeper's face was unsmiling, but then she was unsmiling with everyone, she wasn't picking on Sally.

Kompel gave Sally the smallest packet of sugar on the shelf. "It's the law, Sal," she explained. "See? My mum and dad gets into trouble if they sell cigarettes to kids…"

Sally stared at her, took back the cardboard note with *cigarettes* crossed through, walked out of the shop.

She sighed as she went and her steps were slower than they had been coming. Slower steps, faster heart – because going home without the full message meant she'd done wrong. And doing wrong always got her a good hiding…

From *Sally Cinderella* by Bernard Ashley

Teachers' note Use this in conjunction with the discussion format on page 36. This passage comes from the Clipper Street series, which provides many discussion points for citizenship. These points are drawn out at the end of the story. The children could read the entire book if it is available and continue the discussion to include the interactions between all the characters throughout the story.

Developing Literacy
Speaking & Listening
Year 3
© A & C BLACK

Story characters: 2

- **Discuss the passage from *Sally Cinderella*.**
  How does Sally treat the other characters?
  How do they treat Sally?
- **Fill in the charts.**

Work in a group.

	How Sally treats the other characters
Sally's mum	
Mrs Vasisht	
Kompel	

	How the others treat Sally
Sally's mum	
Mrs Vasisht	
Kompel	

Now try this!

- **How might Sally feel at different points in the passage? Discuss this with your group.**

Teachers' note The children will need to refer to the passage on page 35. Each child could fill in their own copy of this page. Ask them to comment on whether the characters treat one another well, why the children think they behave this way and how this might make the other characters feel (see page 8). They should support their answers with evidence from the passage.

**Developing Literacy
Speaking & Listening
Year 3
© A & C BLACK**

What if...?

- Work in a group.
- Read part of a fiction book together.
- What choices do the characters make?
- What could they have done instead?

Word bank

because   could   if   in case   maybe
might   possibly   should   so
then   whether   why   would

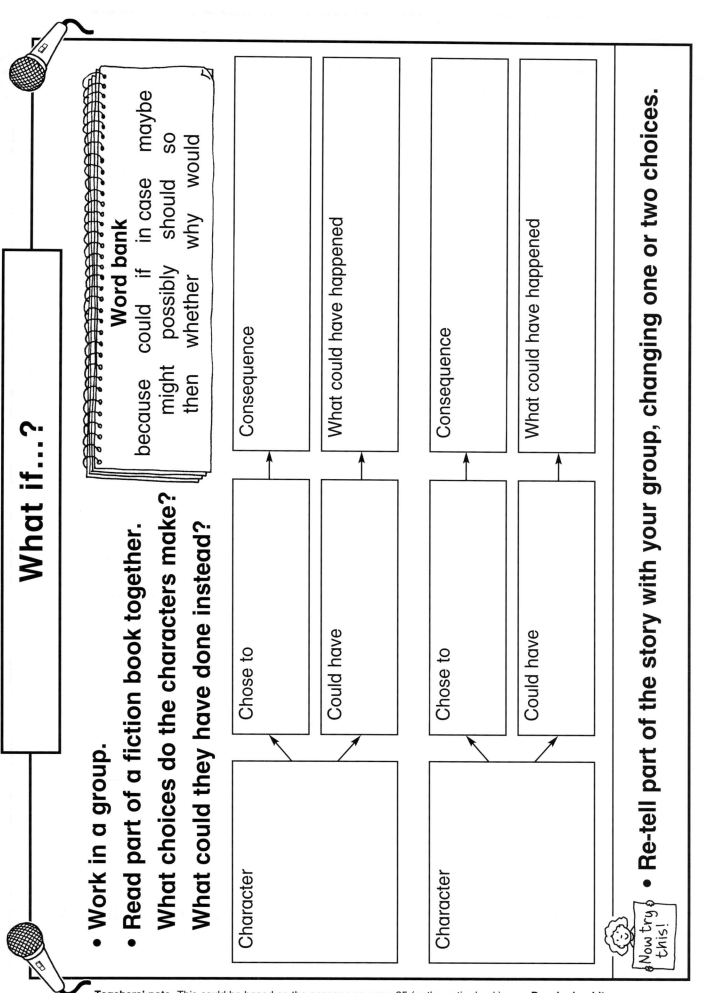

| Character | | Chose to → | Consequence |
| | | Could have → | What could have happened |

| Character | | Chose to → | Consequence |
| | | Could have → | What could have happened |

- Re-tell part of the story with your group, changing one or two choices.

Now try this!

Teachers' note This could be based on the passage on page 35 (or the entire book) or on another book the children have been reading. The children could take turns to act as scribe. Ask them to look for choices and decisions made by the characters and how these affected others, and to discuss what they could have done instead.

**Developing Literacy
Speaking & Listening
Year 3
© A & C BLACK**

Guess who

• Work in a large group.

☆ Get into pairs. Each pair will need a card.

☆ Plan a conversation between the characters on your card.

☆ The others in your group have to guess who you are.

How will you change your voice?

Talk to your partner about this.

snowman and snow woman

bus driver and passenger

traffic warden and driver

police officer and burglar

sheep and sheepdog

Father Christmas and toyshop manager

magician and rabbit

chef and waiter

butterfly and caterpillar

Teachers' note Cut out the cards and give one to each pair of children. You could make the activity easier by letting the children see all the cards and cut them out for themselves. Allow time for discussion and planning in pairs, then ask the children to take turns to enact the dialogue between the characters on their card. It is useful to model with another adult how to speak in role.

**Developing Literacy
Speaking & Listening
Year 3
© A & C BLACK**

Digging up the past

- **Work in a group of four.**
- **Imagine you are four** `archaeologists` **on a dig.**

☆ Cut out the cards.

☆ Take one each.

☆ Take turns to describe your **artefact** to the group.

What does it look like?
What could it have
been used for?

Coins

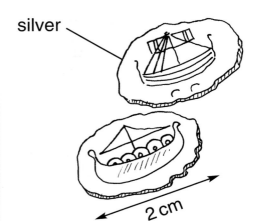

silver

2 cm

Clay pot

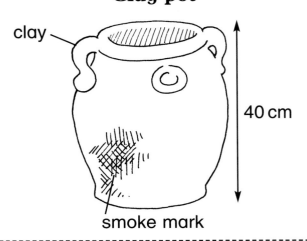

clay

40 cm

smoke mark

Loom weights

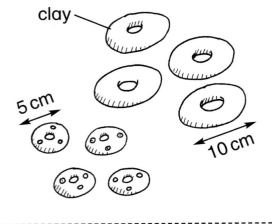

clay

5 cm

10 cm

Stones for grinding flour

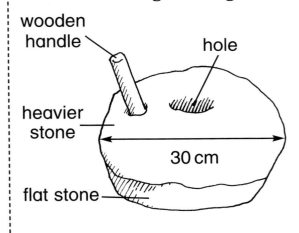

wooden
handle

hole

heavier
stone

30 cm

flat stone

 **Now try this!**

- **Work with a partner.**
- **'Dig up' another artefact. Tell your partner what you can learn from it.**

Teachers' note Link this activity with work in history on invaders and settlers, providing relevant background information. Begin by explaining any terms the children are not familiar with. The children should be encouraged to speak in role as archaeologists. For the extension activity, prepare a mock dig by hiding replica artefacts (or pictures of artefacts) in a tray filled with sand.

**Developing Literacy
Speaking & Listening
Year 3
© A & C BLACK**

Lost in the woods

- **Work in a group of four.**
- **Each choose a character from a book you know well.**
- **Draw your character and make notes about his or her** | personality |.

The characters should be from different books.

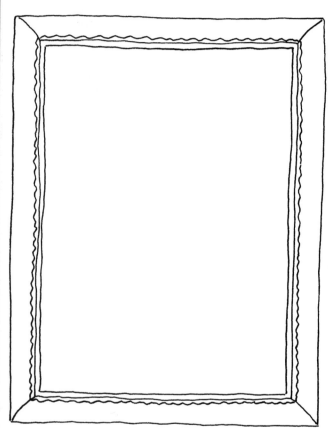

Notes

- **Imagine that these four characters get lost in a forest. What do they do? What do they say? Act the scene with your group.**

How will you keep your audience interested?

Now try this!

- **Imagine that two characters find their way out of the forest. Act the scene.**

Work with a partner.

Teachers' note Provide a selection of books from which the children can choose their characters. Ask them to re-read the book (or parts of it) to remind themselves about their character's personality. When enacting the scene, they should think about how the character might respond to being lost in the forest (see page 8). Link this with work in citizenship on communities and human rights.

Developing Literacy Speaking & Listening Year 3 © A & C BLACK

Imagine a friend asks you to do something wrong:

Patrick

> I'm not speaking to Ella.
> You're *my* friend.
> Don't talk to her.
> Don't play with her.

Lucy

Ella

What would you say?

- **Work with a partner.**

> What will you say to make your audience interested?

- **Act the scene.**

- **Write what you both said.**

- **What other wrong action might someone ask you to do? Act a** dialogue **about it.**

Teachers' note This could develop from work in citizenship lessons on right and wrong. Give the children a few minutes to consider what they might say if they were the friend of Patrick, and why they might not do what they know is right in this situation. Encourage pairs to prepare the dialogue between Patrick and Lucy for an audience. They can take turns to write what they said in the speech bubbles.

**Developing Literacy
Speaking & Listening
Year 3
© A & C BLACK**

Costume drama

- **Choose a film character with an interesting costume.**
- **Draw and label the costume.**

Describe the colours, materials and style.

- **Write a caption.**
  (What is the film? Who is the character? How does the costume show what the character is like?)

_____

_____

_____

_____

_____

Now try this!

- **Imagine two characters swapped costumes. Describe how this would affect the audience.**

Teachers' note This could be based on a television programme or film the children have watched as a group or on one they have watched independently. Ask them to think of a costume which told the audience something about the character wearing it: for example, the furs worn by Cruella De Vil in _101 Dalmatians_, or Superman's outfit.

Developing Literacy
Speaking & Listening
Year 3
© **A & C BLACK**

Actions speak louder

- **Work with a partner.**
- **Cut out the cards.**
- **Match the characters to the descriptions.**

Characters

Descriptions

This man has just got the baby to sleep and is tiptoeing out of the room.	This girl has heard that she has got top grades in her tests.
This boy has been hit and called names by a group of children from his school. He had thought some of them were his friends.	This girl wants her mum to let her stay up late to watch a film on television. She says that all her friends are going to watch it and she will be the only one not allowed.
This keen gardener is telling off his neighbour's children for spoiling his flower bed. He has spent a lot of time caring for this flower bed.	This grandmother has just got off the train and is being met by her grandchildren.

Now try this!

- **Take turns to mime one of the actions in the pictures. Your partner has to guess which it is.**

Teachers' note You could introduce this by showing the children a video of a television drama with the sound turned off. Ask them what feelings the characters are showing, and how they can tell. Focus on the characters' stance or posture, how they move their arms, the angle of their heads and so on.

Developing Literacy
Speaking & Listening
Year 3
© A & C BLACK

43

Face to face

Faces can show feelings.

- **Draw lines to match the characters to the way they are feeling.**

| amused |

| shocked |

| happy |

| sad |

| surprised |

| excited |

- **Act these** facial expressions **with a partner.**
  Tick the feelings your partner shows well.

Work with a partner.

Now try this!

- **Choose three of the feelings. Use them in a role-play with your partner.**

Teachers' note This activity could be introduced by showing a video of cartoons, which exaggerate gestures and facial expressions. Pause the video and ask the children to mimic some of the facial expressions of the characters. Discuss the feelings being portrayed. Pairs who complete the extension activity can perform their role-plays for others to comment on how well they showed the feelings.

Developing Literacy
Speaking & Listening
Year 3
© A & C BLACK

Pass it on

- **Work in a group of four.**
- **Read a verse each and pass on the smile.**

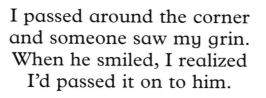

A Smile

Smiling is infectious
you catch it like the flu.
When someone smiled at me today
I started smiling too.

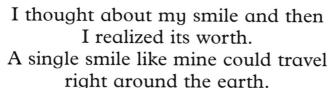

I passed around the corner
and someone saw my grin.
When he smiled, I realized
I'd passed it on to him.

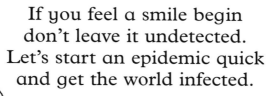

I thought about my smile and then
I realized its worth.
A single smile like mine could travel
right around the earth.

If you feel a smile begin
don't leave it undetected.
Let's start an epidemic quick
and get the world infected.

Jez Alborough

- **How did the poem make you feel?**
  Can you make people feel happy by
  smiling at them? If you feel sad, might
  this make people around you feel sad?

Discuss this with your group.

- **Share your group's thoughts with the rest of the class.**

Now try this!

- **Take turns to pass on an expression:**

| excitement | being bored | being tired |

Teachers' note To introduce this activity, tell the children that they are going to read a poem with their group and then discuss how it makes them feel. Ask the children if they can think of times when their feelings and actions have been influenced by the moods or emotions of people around them.

Developing Literacy
Speaking & Listening
Year 3
© A & C BLACK

Abraham and Sarah

The story of Abraham and Sarah is in the book of Genesis in the Old Testament of the Bible.

• **Read what God said to Abraham.**

Work with a partner.

> Abraham and his wife Sarah lived in a city called Haran. They had no children.
>
> One day, when Abraham was seventy-five years old, God said to him, "Leave your country, your people and your father's household and go to a place which I am going to show you. You will be the father of a great nation, and I shall bless you and make your name so great that it will be used in blessings."

• **Make notes about how you could act the parts of Abraham and Sarah.**
  How might they feel about leaving their home?

How can you show this using your face and body?

Abraham	Sarah

• **Act the dialogue.**

Now try this!

• **Read the next part of the story.**
• **Act it with a partner.**

Genesis chapter 12

Teachers' note This could be introduced during an RE lesson on faith. Ask the children how Abraham might have felt about leaving his home and going off to a strange place. Give the children time to think about this and about how he would broach the subject with Sarah. How might she respond? How would she feel about leaving her family and friends?

Developing Literacy Speaking & Listening Year 3 © A & C BLACK

Victims

- **Work with a partner.**

- **Plan how to act the role of <u>one</u> of the victims:**

  – as their property is stolen

feelings	thoughts

  – later

feelings and worries	thoughts

- **Speak the victim's feelings, worries and thoughts. Speak as if you are the victim.**

- **What is she/he most worried about?**

  > Use 'I' and 'me'.

Now try this!

- **Role-play what happens to the mugger. Does she/he feel guilty? Does she/he get caught?**

Teachers' note After the planning stage, introduce and explain the term 'monologue'. Invite volunteers to speak in the role of the victim. Explain that although victims might not speak all their thoughts in real life, a monologue is useful in drama for expressing thoughts and feelings.

**Developing Literacy
Speaking & Listening
Year 3
© A & C BLACK**

How did you do?

Name _____ **Date** _____

Activity title _____

| **Listening to others** |

- ## What was good about what they said?

_____

_____

- ## What could they have done better?

_____

_____

| **Speaking to others** |

- ## What did you do well?

_____

_____

- ## What could you do better next time?

_____

_____

| **Talking as a group** |

- ## What was good about talking as a group?

_____

_____

- ## What could you all do better next time?

_____

_____

Teachers' note Parts of this could be completed after several activities have been carried out, building up a record of the children's attainment over the course of a term or year. You may wish to remind the children of important speaking skills (such as speaking clearly and remembering to look up) and what makes a successful group discussion (taking turns; listening to and supporting each other).

Developing Literacy
Speaking & Listening
Year 3
© A & C BLACK